M. Maurizio Zucchi

STATISTICAL TRADING
HOW TO GET RESULTS FROM THE CHARTS

This handbook contains everything you need to build a practical strategy (with stoploss and takeprofit) to begin earning statistically. Approaches to these strategies are simple, but those who do not know online trading, especially Forex and Shares, should first read the chapter that is below in a simplified version.

CHAPTER 1 - NOTIONS

THE MARKETS

Trading markets are many, but we can summarize the main ones, those that are of interest to us. They are mainly subdivided into stock markets, indexes and currencies markets. The tools available to trade on these "charts" are many: bonds, stocks, options, and so on. Whatever the market, they all have a common factor: the charts. Charts of the price trend of a stock, currency, stock, etc. are the first thing a trader looks at. Only by that one understands the trend of the market. As a second factor, there will be information about why that trend (for example, an action we will check the budgets, a valuation of information related to it).
In the past, crypto-monies have also entered the field, such as online coins, such as Bitcoin, Litecoin, Dogecoin and so on. Even these coins are traded more or less with the same logic described above, ie graphs + information.
Now, we will focus only on the most practical and easy-to-learn markets, ie buy / sell on charts.

The Forex.

Forex is a very liquid market, among the currencies of countries in the world. Exchanges take place from Sunday evening until Friday forwarded (Italian time), 24 hours a day. The most used platforms traded forex, both for these reasons, and because in the years many people have been keen on this market, and with it brokers have ridden the wave. Forex brokers are distinguished between electronic communication network (ECN) and Market Maker. The first are more reliable, but also more expensive (include additional commissions), the second is the vast majority, and you can also open accounts with a few euros. However, most are unreliable, and they are counterparts to the customer, as in online casinos, when the customer loses, the bank "wins". With this brief premise, you must choose a broker based in a trusted country with many permissions (UK, USA, Australia, etc.). For the rest of the information, please refer to the paragraph above. Additionally, differences in the stock market, where stocks are mainly bought for "multyday" (ie, keeping them for a long time) with forex brokers is not possible, or rather counterproductive. In fact, there are additional night-time commissions called SWAP overnight which have a heavy impact on operations, especially those carried out with leverage. The forex market is more suitable for short or medium term operations.

Stocks&Index (cfd).

The stock includes all the capitalized companies in their market. Indexes are the sum of all the actions treated in that graph. For example, the Nasdaq100 contains the first 100 technology titles made in the US, the DAX all German stocks. The indexes are much more liquid than the shares, but they also have the gap of ordinary closing from 5.30 pm to 8 am to 9 am, heavily limiting their operations. Actions have some additional factor to keep in check, mainly news about the company (budgets, mergers, etc.) that may have a major impact on the trend. In general, even here, for those who make day trading and close all day or almost, follow the charts and above all the trend of the main indexes. Because of commissions and liquidity factors, the stock market is the least attractive market for the strategy we will see later.

The cryptomarkets.

For some years, he has taken on a new financial instrument, ie virtual coins, such as Bitcoins, Litecoins, Dogecoins, and so on. These are markets in all respects, with thousands if not millions of exchanges every day. Unfortunately, these markets are still not well regulated, and in the cryptocoins jungle it is easy to get cheated. We talk about thefts to accounts, to fraudsters brokers who close from day to day with all customer currencies. However, being a new and fashionable market, there are many brokers, who are spinning like mushrooms, some with serious intentions to carry out the projects. The cryptocoins are traded as the most extreme and inexpensive stockpile, the American pennystock, capable of periods where nothing happens, until the arrival of the hoped news that sparks the price, sometimes at 1000% in just one day. It is clear that with such performances you can earn or lose a lot of money. As a management of the approach, the rules of a share are worthwhile, that is to keep news and graphics handy. As for the more "liquid" markets, the Bitcoin, the most famous and most traded currency among them, can even be traded as "day trading" by looking at charts. That is, there are many occasions during almost every day. Unlike the less famous and therefore less liquid, they have to be bought and kept "waiting" for a possible price explosion in the best times.

Commissions.

One of the most important aspects to focus on is commissions. Almost all brokers ask for a commission each time you do a trading deal, both on purchase and on sale. You will first have to do the servant's accounts. An example. Close an operation to +3 euros knowing that you will spend 4 euros on commissions does not make much sense of business. Make fast operations like scalping on markets that have large commissions, so it's a waste of time and money!

Although some brokers do not have commissions but hold a "portion" of your transaction (called spreads) is in effect a commission, and you must always check that the chart we are operating is not excessive for our trading.

WHICH MARKET CHOOSES.

Whether it's a stock market, currency, commodity, etc. The graphics are almost the same. They have lateral movements, up or down. These movements are called trend, and can last days, months or years depending on the scale you look at the graph (called timeframe or TF).

The markets on which to trade in first-rate weapons are obviously simpler. You have to focus on your habits first: a "multyday" trading will mean that you will remain in the position (purchase or sale) for a few or many days, and if you are better off with a frantic trading, you can choose day trading or open and close positions within a day. In some cases of extreme trading, called scalping, positions are also closed after a few minutes or seconds. To find out the trading style you like, you just have to try the different disciplines with your demo account.

THE PLATFORM.

To buy and sell we need a trading platform that can be combined with a current account or a broker, which usually does both of these things. Internet brokers are many, but you have to be careful because many of these are not always clear and you have to be careful about certain factors.

The factors to be considered are: a tax office and operating in a country that does not "defend" the interests of the broker. That is, the headquarters are in a serious country and with controlled bodies. USA, UK, Australia and Italy have control bodies, so brokers who are based here are very confident. Another factor to consider is solidity. A known broker and market for years is more difficult than it is unreliable. Check on the web any reviews, but wide range. Remember that it is very easy to create fake reviews!

The first thing to do once you find the right broker is to open a demo account, which is nothing more than a fake cash account and start practicing with the platform. Opening the demo account is always free, you have to fill in a form with email to which you will send the login credentials. In many cases you can also decide how much money you will have the account. Remember that this is fake money!

WHAT IS THE LEVERAGE?

As mentioned before, all transactions are performed using borrowed money. This allows you to take advantage of the lever. Leverage 200: 1 allows you to trade 1,000 euros in the market by setting aside only € 5 as a security deposit. This means that you can also leverage the smallest currency movements by controlling more money in the market than what's in your account. On the other hand, leverage can significantly increase your losses. FOREX trading with any leverage may not be suitable for all types of investors.

The exact amount you set aside for each open position is defined as the required margin. This margin can be compared to a security deposit on open positions. It's not a commission or a transaction fee, but just a small part of your bill set as a guarantee deposit.

MAKE THE FIRST ORDER.

Placing an order on the market is simple. All you have to do is click on the purchase or sale price you want to negotiate in the "Display Price" window. Then, simply, it is confirmed by clicking "OK".
Step 1: Click on "BUY" (buy) or on "SELL" (sell)
Step 2: Click "OK" to confirm

MONITOR ACTIVE POSITIONS.

When there are open positions in the market you need to know what's going on, if these positions are in profit or loss. To do this, just check the "Accounts" window of the Trading Station. In this window all open positions and details are presented.

CLOSE OPEN POSITIONS.

When you are ready to close an open position, just click on the appropriate price on the "Sell and Close" column or "Buy and Close" column of the

"Summary" window. At this point, you can confirm the details of the order by clicking "OK". Once the position is closed, the corresponding profit (or loss) will be recorded and the balance of the account will be updated accordingly in the "Account" window. It should be remembered that the balance of the account only relates to the profits and losses actually consolidated. The total position value, however, is the balance plus the possible profits or losses of the open positions.

HOW TO READ A CHART.

Forex traders have developed several methods to find out the direction of the exchange rate. Traders relying on fundamental analysis methods use research to identify how demand and supply of a currency are affected by interest rates, economic growth, employment rate, inflation, and risk from the situation policy. Traders who, on the contrary, rely on technical analysis use graphical methods and analytical indicators to identify the trends and the correct price level to enter or exit the market. That said, however, it is absolutely important that whatever your specific orientation is, you learn to read the charts.

OPEN A CHART.

To start, click on the "create chart" button located at the top of the Trading Station screen. After this, we have to choose a pair of currencies, choose the time period, and define the date range.

The timeframe is the time range interval that is updated on the graph. For example, if the period is 1 day, each point in the graph represents a full day of trading; if you choose 5 minutes each point contains the data collected in 5 minutes. The date range is the amount of data needed to populate the chart. For example, if you want to see the trend for a year, you have to choose just one year interval.

USE CANDLESTICK IN A CHART.

The default type of charts is that called "candles." This type of chart is used very frequently on Forex. A bar (element representing a chronological interval, may be one minute as a month, or any other time interval), or candle, in a candle chart shows the minimum, maximum, opening, and closing in the range of selected time. The candle body is between opening and closing, while the line (called "wick" or "wake") is between the minimum and the maximum.

ADD AN INDICATOR.

Examining a candle chart can provide useful information to make a trading decision, however, many traders add to this basic chart one (or more) technical indicators to further support the decision. These tools are useful to the trader, as they help you locate price trends and predict future price trends. There are then over 600 indicators among the most popular or specialist that can be downloaded via the web.

DESIGN A TRENDLINE.

Prices may have a tendency to grow (called "bullish"), to remain constant (called "lateral") or to decrease (called "bearish"). A "trendline" helps the trader to see the direction in which the trend moves (normally the trend lines represent resistances and DYNAMIC support). Until there is evidence of a break in a trend, the trader can logically expect the trend to continue. Trend lines are drawn with the "add line" tool. Usually, trend lines are traced by connecting two or more maximum (Dynamic Resistance Line) or two or more (Dynamic Support Line).

STRATEGIES.

A strategy is needed to make a profit. After having practiced and gained confidence in the trading platform, a trading strategy must be studied. This strategy (or more strategies) will have to be tested on the field, on the demo account with fake money, for at least a few months, realizing if they can make sense with real money. The strategies, to be successful, must meet certain questions that we will have:

What is My Strategy Based? (For example, an entry on a given price level);

What happens in a negative time to our account? (Called jumbo draws);

How much can one earn or lose on each single operation?

Can we replicate it with real money on a real account? (psychological factor);
What if a price explosion occurs? (News, unexpected news, etc.).
These are the main questions you need to answer, but there are many more. The important thing about your trading method will be to have an answer to any problem you will be presenting, so you do not stay bogged down.

The ways to create an ad hoc strategy are almost infinite, but you need to know that markets are changing over time, and a winning strategy today may not be in the future. It is therefore important to diversify on different strategies, and above all to look at historical charts, in order to see how the strategy was used in the past. Typically, strategies also use price indicators that you will default to on your broker. These indicators draw on the chart some past price features and can often give useful information but do not trust too much.
The best way is to invent and experiment with different strategies (some free and user-shared strategies found on forums online such as forexfactory.com or forums for Italian forex) and after trying them different, deepen your talk with what you find better . Doing tests, understanding

why you gain / lose a strategy and all its factors will be your battle horse!

THE MONEYMANAGEMENT.

In close connection with the strategist, there is risk management. On each trading platform you can choose how many contracts, shares, lots, and so on, you can buy. The important thing to know is the percentage of risk. Setting a 10% stop loss is not the best if you are not trader with particular markets. It's just a week or a little more negative, and your account will drop to zero.
If I charge a maximum of 1% per day, I know that in theory I can drain my account in 100 days of negative days. Considering that there will also be positive days and statistically closing 100 negative days in a row, it is statistically unlikely, as a percentage sounds better. But you can do it even better, it depends on your experience of market statisticians. If I have a few historical mistakes, I could dare to buy more contracts, but if I have little information, I dare to cheat less, and maybe try to close a profit.

The relationship between potential gain / sale is called risk reward jargon. In theory the gain must be ever greater than the loss, with this statistical trick your earnings should increase over time. But on the practical side it is not always true. If you do casual or unsuccessful transactions, the distribution of the "weights" in the trading will bring you, considering commissions, a 48% victory and 52% losses. The argument is true even if you use a 1: 5 risk reward, for example, with a risk of 1 and a potential profit of 5. On the long run, you will have 4 locked-down operations and one in 5 for profit, so a 50 and 50 return, less commissions.

It is evident that without a proper and winning strategy, risk reward does not make sense. One needs to find an appetizing market situation and trade it.

Summary.
Now that you've learned how trading in general works, you can move more smoothly into the jungle of this world, full of pitfalls.

To begin, follow these steps:

1 Understanding and market choice (shares, Cfd or currencies);

2 Choosing the right broker (search on Google, and evaluate the broker's goodness);

3 Choice of strategy after months of demo tests;

4 Once you are familiar with a strategy, always deepen your demo until you have good results, even by looking back at the charts that the strategy regresses.
5 Diversify with other strategies and always run new tests.

CHAPTER 2 - OPERATING

HOW TO GET RESULTS FROM GRAPHICS: STATISTICS-MATHEMATICS AND NEWS.

They are the key components. I would also add the commission side, that is, before doing a trade, observe the spread, the overnight policy (swap) and the commissions of your broker. If all of these are high, there is no point in making certain operations (such as scalping, or chassis positions, etc.). Made this premise, and taking into account the commissions (a few lines to keep in mind), we will focus on the three "pillars" to start earning over time by observing a chart. We go in order of importance.

STATISTICS

Statistics are a key factor in obtaining profits over time. There are several statistical factors, such as historians, or those applied to a chart. If we look at any chart of any product, as we have seen in the small beginner's manual, we will have different situations, but three main ones: horizontal trend, bullish trend (upward) or bearish trend (downward). So the price determines a line that goes only in these three directions. If we analyze a lateral trend that moves to zigzag, it is easy to guess where we need to place an order: at the end of this side channel, both at the top and the bottom. These are the key points in reading the chart. Placing an order at that point could give us a statistical advantage over the long run. But that's not enough. We have to put aside various statistical factors before we get good results. Chart view is fundamental. You have to check how many times the trend is lateral and how many up / downs. The chart should be read almost and only in the timeframe we are going to buy, as we will use take profit and stoploss. If the chart often appears on the side, we will often use trades versus trend: now imagine a lateral trend with zig zag price. If we get to the extremes it will be profitable to enter against trend to exploit the various inversions at the end of the channel. If, on the other hand, there is a graph mainly for long up /

down trends, we will pick up an oblique channel with inputs at the bottom of the channel, in favor of the price. Now that we have the input and the characteristics of the chart, there is only to see the risk profit, that is to set a proper performance risk. If, for example, on a currency pair, we use a timeframe, we will have to use a stoploss of at least 40-50 pips, so it covers any useless price fluctuations. Using the same stoploss on a retail chart will not be possible, at least that there are no particular conditions of price explosions that alter the chart. Then adjusting the stoploss to the charts as a form of "camouflage" is a key factor. But what risk-profit should we use? Depends on the chart. But in general, it is always good to use a lower risk, so with a ratio of 1: 2 (risk = 1 yield = 2), for example. Such a rule, applied to these key input points, will give us, in the long run, a gain. Not all markets are, however, suitable. As a rule, you always have to keep in mind that the market meets certain requirements, such as good moves, which make us take the take profit. Inserting a 50-point takeprofit, on a channel that moves at most 20, does not make much sense! So first you have to analyze the graph and the entry points as described above.

MATH

In addition to the previous chapter, let us now analyze the mathematical factor. We have graphs, revenue and also risk-yielding. We almost ride! Let's try to analyze some combinations of risk performance using our favorite, that is risk =1 profit =2.

Situation 1, random revenue, without taking into account the supports, resistances, and so on. Statistical distribution 50-50 less commissions and spreads.

Lost Trades = 7
Trades won = 3
Gain = -1

Situation 2, with reasoned inputs on supports / resistances.

Lost Trades = 4
Trades won = 6
Gain = +8

Situation 3, as before but with more unfavorable graphics.

Lost Trades = 7

Trades won = 3
Gain = -1

Situation 4, balance.

Trades lost = 5
Trades won = 5
Gain = 5

As we have seen, maintaining a simple risk / profit ratio of 1 to 2, we get amazing results, if you think a little about the revenue. Only in the worst case, where almost all trades were wrong (it may happen for certain periods) there was a loss, and really ridiculous, of -1. In all other cases, even a substantial draw or trades number lost slightly higher than those won, there was always a gain. In the situation 1 we wanted to include a random example to make it clear that if we do not give a reason for the entry point, if we do not put a favorable condition on our part, it is not enough to have a positive risk / profit to earn (otherwise it would be too easy !). The statistical distribution, whatever your risk / profit, before or after, leads to a situation of equality between earnings and losses, namely 50%, less commissions. That is, in our example, 7 trades went wrong and 3 went well. Total = -1. This is not just a practical example, but could include years of statistical distribution. Statistics say that by trading at random, with any risk / profit you will have a good chance of having positive and negative periods, but without a real advantage. These are extreme situations, because anyone looking for a statistical approach by looking at a chart. Even a neophyte, looking at a chart that now has a "low line" would buy long, rather than a short. A trivial example, but it makes sense that any person tries a sort of statistical approach.

NEWS

This chapter is less important than others, because it mainly concerns stock markets, or at the limit, even cryptocoins and forex, if you use lower timeframes. The news is, however, important, and to keep an eye on. Starting from the assumption that knowing the direction of a news is very difficult, it is because many times are manipulated by large investors, because when we get to know the news, that has given its impact on the price and chart already for a few minutes. News in Cryptomonas and Forex should therefore be used as a warning to stay away from the market near their exit, especially if they are not experienced and specialized news traders.

In the shareholder, however, especially at medium or higher timeframes, one must keep an eye on. As news we obviously mean budgets about the company, mergers and so on. The experienced trader evaluates all these factors, in addition to the chart. So if on the Forex currency market, important news warns us not to enter the market, the shareholder, and sometimes in the cryptocoins, they should be taken into account for any purchases. The technique we describe, on supports and resistances, and which we have already mentioned, if used on medium timeframes (TF H1 or H4), does not have any particular contraindications even in the presence of news. Also because most of the prices are followed by the charts, rather than the news (hence, because of inexplicable movements on news considered "certain", they have found "frigates" to the practical effect of the release of the news, going in the opposite direction of where it was thought). So you have to focus on graphics, statistics and math, as we have seen before.

CHAPTER 3 - THE STRATEGY

The strategy we propose is very simple. It is about placing pending orders, with pre-set takeprofit and stoploss. Usually, with the following values:
TP = 100 points
SL = 50 points
That is, a risk-return 1:2 in favor of the latter. This is the basic rule, but these values can also be noticed. For example, if in a side channel we put a pendant on the top, at the maximum price levels, maybe you will not need to have a standard stoploss of 50 points, just let the stoploss line be some point higher than the maximum price reached . In total, then, maybe our stop will be 20 points. At this point, we will not need a 100-point standard take-up, which is difficult to achieve with these targets. So we will choose for the usual 1: 2 risk reward, in plain words, a take profit of 40 or 60 if there are enough assumptions.

Placements.
Pending orders should be placed in three chart situations. Horizontal (or lateral) chart, bullish trend (upward oblique channel) and bearish trend (oblique channel down). Each pattern (so called these figures) will have different strategy situations, but once you learn the three figures, they will always be the same.

Below you can see the three situations and their inputs.

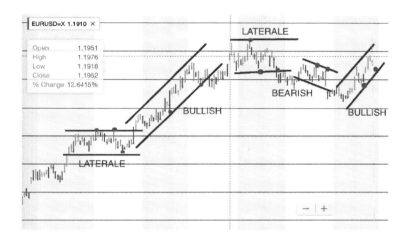

As you can see, in a bullish trend, the pendants should be positioned at the bottom of the "channel". In the bearish trend the opposite occurs, the pendants are placed in the upper part. In the lateral trend, both high and low. The rules are very simple. The important thing is to respect the maximum / minimum price achieved by the figure, and the risk reward.

The advantage of using hanging orders is very advantageous. First, because you do not have to follow every trade in your pc, just take a look every now and then (see why), secondly, because the statistical factor materializes with the ordered orders: if at a given minimum level we place a pendant, we know once the price reaches that value, it will usually happen something. Investors know how you know that that level is important, so they will invest in that franchise. Two situations may occur.

Trade will go into the port and then you will earn 2. Trade will take an unexpected situation and then you will lose 1.

In any case, on 10 lost trades, it will be enough to recover 5. But this is not the goal. The objective is the statistic, that is to check back the figures and note, as explained above where there will be statistical advantages. If, when forming side channels, we simulate the inputs at the extremes, and note that we would bring 8 winners on 12, we're on horseback. We will have 16 apples and 4 lost apples (risk reward 1 = 2). And do not think that such situations are so difficult. If you trade at random, or unmitigated, perhaps at market level, as 90% of first-time traders do, it's clear that you have bad scenarios, with 7-8 trades lost and 1-2 won. It's a normal thing, price moves almost at random. But if we sit with pendants, then by eliminating the initial psychological factor, and only where there are statistical occasions (precisely at the extremes of the channels described above), we will have for strengths of things, positive results over time. Just take a look at any chart, draw two lines and pretend to enter the extremes, to realize it. Opportunities on average timeframes (h1-h4) are many. Of course, you have to practice in identifying the figures.

How to find channels.
Identifying the input channels is not difficult, but a bit of practice is needed. We've seen that there are only 3 situations.

Side channel.
When the price (chart) begins to move sideways, as soon as it forms a maximum and a minimum, we will skip two horizontal lines as shown in the figure. If the channel is truly horizontal, it will remain within these values. The pendants, let's remember, should be placed in the lower-high part of the channel, SELL in the top, BUY in that low.

EUR/JPY close:**128.78645**

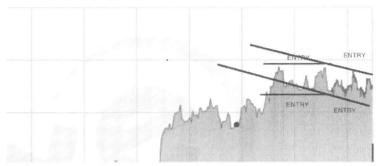

Side channel that turns into a mild bearish channel. Allow us to make entries both on top and bottom lines. When the price gets a real trend we will use the channels explained below.

Bullish Channel.

After a break up of a side channel, it is very likely that a bullish trend will occur. Usually after the break, the trend will trace down slightly, then push will make it new. At this point, sketch two oblique lines on the max-minima of this channel. The pendants, let's remember, should be placed at the bottom of the channel, all BUY.

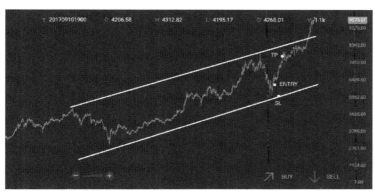

The bullish channel on bitcoin. Once the channel is located, the stop is placed around the lower line. The TP will be the double / triple stop.

Bearish Channel.
Same argument of the bullish but in reverse.
After a break down of a side channel, it is very likely that a bearish trend will occur. Usually after the break, the trend will retract upwards for a little, then push will make it new. At this point, sketch two oblique lines on the max-minima of this channel. The pendants, let's remember, should be placed at the top of the channel, all SELL.

USD to JPY Chart

Bearish Channel. Inputs are placed on the top line, with external stop. TP which are the double / triple of the latter.

When the figure (pattern) does not respect the max/min of the channel, it is good not to work:

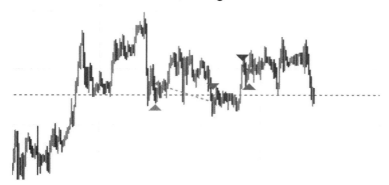

In the figure, the trend appears initially sideways, but the minimum is broken, though the price remains in the area. In these uncertain cases, it is best not to run the strategy, or at best, to position yourself at the extremes with a very close stop, as the chances of winning are slim.

Which timeframe to use.

It is useful to use intermediate timeframes, more generally, the timeframe h1 or h4. The important thing is, on average, that orders have stops on the 50 default maximum points. Using these timeframes, the figures are more reliable, and the spreads and commissions costs are duly debited, with minimal impact.

How to handle the position.

Once the trade is gaining (our forecast was right), it may be helpful to handle the position. This is especially true when you have some practice, otherwise you leave default stoploss and take profit. On the other hand, simulating the trades on the charts, you have noticed that the trades would be statistically traded without ever touching the stoploss. However, once the trade has reached 40-50% of the target, it is useful to move the stoploss in equal, or at some point of profit (this technique is called "break even"). If you do not feel safe on the price / chart (note that it's hard to reach the target set) you can put the stoploss a dozen points behind the price, with the tick at the trailing stop (in practice that stop will follow the price, always keeping a distance of 10 points). Both of these practices are very relaxing, as at most, if you get to the stoploss, in the worst cases, you will not miss anything, otherwise you will get a good profit (though not all of the predefined).

PRACTICAL EXAMPLES

Let's analyze the results of a possible portion of the chart. We will use a performance risk around 1: 2, so take profits will be almost double the stoploss. Obviously, and this also applies to the previous chapter, the risk-performance ratio is recommended for the latter (yield), but stoploss does not necessarily have to be a fixed number, it may be adjusted according to the chart. The important thing is that the take profit is much higher than the loss.

From the graphic image, we can see how to proceed. After some price movements, we will locate the channel. In the first case on the left, channel 1 is bullish, up, so we will use a dynamic support line just below the channel. Around this zone (it does not have to be exactly on the line, we can leave some junk points) we will place our pendants with a risk-profit 1 = 2. In the example, a stoploss was used around 30 points, and a profit take around 60. Using the "channel" technique, which we will deepen, we almost always went to take profit, except when end of channel 1, there was a reversal and a new trend, in this lateral case, which took shape. Each time a new trend is formed, you will inevitably accuse a loss, as the technique is trend-following. Little if we analyze data risk reward. 5 profits and 1 stop equals, with a loss-yield ratio of 1 = 2, about 10 apples versus 1. If we did not use any stoploss, as we see in the figure, our loss would be magnified around the end of second trend, number 2. Here the price would go down, probably wiping out all the positive results previously collected. Here is the importance of a positive risk-profit: you earn as much in the favorable terms, and contain losses during drawdowns, always by using a strategy with a logic, and a statistic as described above. Let's now look at a less favorable situation with more difficult graphics.

The figure shows a graph that is currently difficult to interpret. After a downward trend, a lateral phase began. At this point, around half the channel, we position the lines on the highest and lowest. The first trade goes well (OK), while the second and probably the third lose. Actually, the second trade, if we left a 50-point stop and a 100-take profit, we would have gained, but the logic is to place the stop on the tops, a few more points, so as to lose as little as possible in terms of points. In any case, even in a negative situation like the one shown in the figure, our "math control" thanks to risk reward 1: 2 brings us home a peer. That is, 2 losses and a take profit. Not bad, although the figure was not the best. Let's see another situation.

In this case favorable, you know how to act. Find the maximum and minimum of the first channel, the side one, proceed with the first order, which brings us gain, then the second one sell, this also gains gain. At this point the trend changes, having broken the minima. Expecting the lateral channel dynamic resistance, and as soon as it is configured, you enter the maximum. Another chance. The latest trade, cataloged as a loss (NO) although in theory we have to leave some margin points, if we use a stop of a dozen points, it really brings us a loss. So 3 out of 4, which bring a good gain. At this point, always using risk-reward 1: 2. To lose all the gain of this figure, they would serve another 5 trades lost in a row!

SUMMARY.

Locate, through the max / min of the pattern, the side / bullish / bearish channel;
Use medium timeframes, type h1 or h4;
Place the pendants in the bottom line of the bullish channels, in the top line in the bearish channels and both in the lateral trend;
Always use stop and take profit;
In the pendant, the stoploss will be at least half of the take profit. The stop will be positioned beyond the line. The take profit will be double or more, the stop.
When the price reaches 30-40% of the target, move the stoploss in equal or positive (break even);
When the price reaches 70% and beyond the target, place a trailing stop just below the price;
In uncertain graphic situations, do not operate.
Use proper money management (leverage 1: 1 max 1: 3).

Recommended Markets: Bitcoin, Forex, Raw Materials.

At this point, after reading and reviewing this manual, you can try a demo account for a few weeks / months, depending on your profitability on the charts. Only then can you open your real counterpart and start with real money. Remember to use the appropriate leverage, and above all be informed about the chosen broker. Good trading!

Portfolio Statement

Date from: 01.11.2017   Date to: 28.11.2017   By Month   Detail level: Daily Summary   Show only days with balance change   Reload   Print   Export

Date	Trading P&L	Commission	Incoming transfers	Outgoing transfers	Balance Change	Balance
09.11.2017	1.42 EUR	-1.00 EUR	10,000.00 EUR	0.00 EUR	10,000.42 EUR	10,000.42 EUR
10.11.2017	123.08 EUR	-0.78 EUR	0.00 EUR	0.00 EUR	122.30 EUR	10,122.72 EUR
13.11.2017	167.04 EUR	-3.46 EUR	0.00 EUR	0.00 EUR	163.58 EUR	10,286.30 EUR
14.11.2017	-61.91 EUR	-5.36 EUR	0.00 EUR	0.00 EUR	-67.27 EUR	10,219.03 EUR
15.11.2017	65.76 EUR	-1.06 EUR	0.00 EUR	0.00 EUR	64.70 EUR	10,283.73 EUR
16.11.2017	-3.26 EUR	-0.26 EUR	0.00 EUR	0.00 EUR	-3.52 EUR	10,280.21 EUR
17.11.2017	206.01 EUR	-1.91 EUR	0.00 EUR	0.00 EUR	204.10 EUR	10,484.31 EUR
20.11.2017	-7.33 EUR	-1.30 EUR	0.00 EUR	0.00 EUR	-8.63 EUR	10,475.68 EUR
21.11.2017	-0.35 EUR	-4.56 EUR	0.00 EUR	0.00 EUR	-4.91 EUR	10,470.77 EUR
22.11.2017	191.92 EUR	-2.42 EUR	0.00 EUR	0.00 EUR	189.50 EUR	10,660.27 EUR
23.11.2017	-34.53 EUR	-0.83 EUR	0.00 EUR	0.00 EUR	-35.36 EUR	10,624.91 EUR
24.11.2017	30.08 EUR	-0.86 EUR	0.00 EUR	0.00 EUR	29.22 EUR	10,654.13 EUR
27.11.2017	108.83 EUR	0.00 EUR	0.00 EUR	0.00 EUR	108.83 EUR	10,762.96 EUR
28.11.2017	-8.84 EUR	-1.09 EUR	0.00 EUR	0.00 EUR	-9.93 EUR	10,753.03 EUR
Total EUR	777.92 EUR	-24.89 EUR	10,000.00 EUR	0.00 EUR	10,753.03 EUR	

Example of Equity about this strategy.
Account: 10k dollars.

Leverage 1:1 per trade.
Stoploss: from 10 to 50 pips max.
TakeProfit: from 30 to 100 max.

32770598R00023

Printed in Great Britain
by Amazon